Hey Mom

Remember to Take Care of You

Tanna Abraham

To my son Caden and the village of loving, helpful, and supportive individuals that co-parent with me.

TABLE
OF CONTENTS

Introduction

INTRODUCTION

About four years ago, in an effort to force my then 5-year-old son Caden to be a little independent-- okay, maybe that was the end goal but in the spirit of keeping it real, I was running late and needed him to get himself dressed that morning. I laid out all his things and instructed him on what to do. Caden was both shocked and appalled. I explained that we were running behind, and I needed him to be a big boy and help himself. Ignoring the fact that I asked him to get himself ready for school, Caden kept asking me to assist him. Again, I reiterated to Caden that we were running behind, and I needed him to be a big boy and help himself. A few seconds later, after pondering my response, Caden looked at me with a serious but concerned look and said, "Did you forget?"

With a puzzled expression on my face I asked, "Forget what?"

"Did you forget you're my mommy?"

I bolted over with laughter after hearing his response. Caden, however, stood there as serious as ever. I assured Caden that I did not abandon my parental duty to him. I told him part of being a good mommy is to foster his independence by stepping back and allowing him to do things for himself. Caden wasn't too thrilled with my response but he went on and got dressed.

His question reminded me of one of my favorite books as a child, Are You My Mother? The book written by P.D. Eastman and edited by Dr. Seuss tracks the journey of a baby bird whose egg hatched while his mother went out to get food for him. Though he is aware that he has a mother, he has no idea what she looks like, so he steps out of his nest to find her. During his journey, he encounters all sorts of animals and machines and asked the question, "Are you my mother?" I found the story amusing as a child but as a parent, I find the story compelling.

Yes! I am aware at all times I am a mother, but my attitude and feelings are sometimes as transient as the story of the hatchling in search of his mother. There was a time when the stressors of life would burden me down so much that I would feel like the old car, barely getting by. Or like the hen, crowing away in frustration. Or like the enormous power shovel, just functioning and laboring from day-to-day.

The role of parenting, whether solely or alongside someone, is an adventure that's filled with lots of joy, laughter, and fulfillment. But it's also a journey that can be weary, emotionally taxing, and cumbersome. I wrote this book for the mom who can admit she has spent a much longer time in the bathroom than needed just to have some quiet time. I wrote this book for the mom who leaves her kids at home with a sitter to run errands but gets carried away by freedom and returns home well past the three hours requested. I wrote this book for the mom who has blamed seasonal allergies for the tears running down her face. I wrote this book for the mom who wears gym clothes every day but never has time to work out. And yes, I wrote this book for the mom who seemingly got this all figured out and is wondering what's the rest of us fussing about.

My prayer is that by the end of the book your sons and daughters will fully recognize you as their mommy, not because you make the pancake with the mickey mouse face. Or because you know exactly which clothes to layout on a particular day. Or because your pickup schedule is better than Uber or Lyft. Your sons and daughters would recognize you as their mommy because you have spent time working on, doing for, taking care of... YOU. Which is huge because that's usually the last person on the list of people you take care of...that's if your name even made the list.

The Power of the Group

If you're wondering why I chose to write a book with a group processing model it's because I've discovered what someone once called, 'The Power of the Group". At my previous church, we held Life Groups which were small groups separated by affinities that focused on a particular book. One Saturday, the group leaders gathered to meet prior to the start of the new season. While sharing and discussing best practices, one gentleman got up and began to talk about "The Power of the Group". He explained unique healing comes, not from the words of a facilitator or words from a book, but from processing that occurs within the group.

In my time of facilitating small groups, I have found the most powerful words someone utters are "Me too". And the most powerful feeling someone has felt is when they realize that they are not alone. The "power of the group" provides a safe space for us to bring our authentic selves, unashamed, unapologetic, and open. To experience the true power of the group, the side-eye must return to its centered position. The shade must return underneath the palm trees and the judgment must return to the courtroom. Yes, you can read the book alone, but I would encourage you to find or create a book club or find a reading partner.

INSTRUCTIONS FOR READING THE BOOK

The book carries a seven-day schedule over the course of 6 weeks:

Day 1: Reading & Processing

This is the day you will read the chapter and process the information. Think of how it resonates with you. Recall similar experiences that you've had. Unearth the buried feelings. This will prepare you for the journaling assignment.

Days 2-6: Journaling

There is a journaling assignment for each day that stems from the chapter. Set aside at least 15 minutes to respond to the journaling prompt for the day.

Day 7: Reflection

It's only fitting that once you've read and journaled you will allow yourself the time to reflect. I've included coloring pages, which I've found is a good activity to do while reflecting. Also, on my website (www.tannaabraham.com) you will find a link to download meditation music to accompany your time of reflection.

Additionally, there are some activities sprinkled throughout the book. I encourage you to do them as well. You will be surprised by how a seemingly simple activity will initiate introspective thoughts and processing. I know how hectic our schedules can be, I can't begin to tell you how many times I've started a book and not finished it. For that reason, you will find that I kept the chapters short but, rest assure you will still find them to be meaningful. I don't want this to be another book you read and talk about a few times but never have a lasting impact on your life. Real change comes when we are willing to put in the work. I think today is a good day to get started. Don't you?

Activity: Tree of Fulfillment

Branches: Write the names of the people that are dependent on you (children, spouse, etc.)

Trunk: List your support systems

Ground: List the things that keep you grounded

After filling in the spaces, take your colored pencils and draw leaves on the tree based on how you feel presently as a parent. E.g. If you feel fulfilled draw a tree that is full and vibrant. If you feel depleted, your tree might only have a few leaves on it. If you feel half or partially fulfilled, then the tree will only have half of its leaves.

WEEK 1

Hey Mom

How Are You?

HEY MOM, HOW ARE YOU?

I will never forget my first ultrasound. I was worried, scared and alone. As a matter of fact, I ended the relationship I was in because it wasn't suitable for me and I realized it was an act of rebellion in my frustration with God. Even after going back to church, attending bible study, and rededicating my life to God, I'd gotten to a point in life where it seemed like everyone around me was doing fine. They were living the way they wanted to live, while I was experiencing struggle after struggle. I had finally reached a point of surrender only to find out a few weeks later I was pregnant.

Once I received the news, I went into a deep depression. Yes, I wanted to be a mom, but not like this. I cried for days as I anticipated the drastic changes that would take place in my life. Then one day, in the midst of my depressive state, I felt a striking pain in my lower abdomen. For the first time since finding out I was pregnant, my thoughts shifted to the concern of my unborn baby. It was at that moment I realized my connection to the baby growing inside of me. My love followed shortly after. The pain continued so I scheduled a doctor's appointment.

Later that day, while in the middle of the ultrasound, I saw the little image of my baby on the screen, moving around as freely as he could. The doctor said, "I think he's having a party in there." In that moment I realized that my baby had no clue of the guilt, shame, worry, and fear that I was feeling; He was simply being. That evening as I sat on the beach staring at the sonogram of my baby, I decided to do everything I could to ensure that my baby would be okay and that we would have a great life. I learned to forget about my feelings and focus solely on him.

While writing this book I realized, in order to truly answer the question, "How are you", you must first revisit the point where you stopped answering the question honestly and/or when you stopped answering it for yourself. The day of my ultrasound was the day I stopped answering the question for myself; I answered the question based on my circumstance and based on how everything was going with my baby.

If I asked you how you were doing right now, how much thought would you actually put into your response? Would you give me a quick 'good' because that's' the standard response, or because that's what you were taught to say, or because everything around you were intact? Would you answer honestly, for yourself? What I've come to realize about that question is that it carries a certain level of vulnerability with it. And the problem is, in our society the question is asked in a fleeting manner, oftentimes out of politeness rather than genuine concern. Sometimes not even waiting for a response, as though it was a rhetorical question. Whether you're asking the question to yourself or to someone else, the essence of the question requires you to stop and feel. It also requires you to ask follow-up questions.

In the first quarter of 2020, our lives as we knew it changed. We found ourselves in the midst of a pandemic that left us all indoors. To make matters worse, I was laid off just a few weeks in from a job that I loved and dedicated much of my time to. It was my dream position. I had a great team, a great manager and I got to travel often. I was also serving on the ministerial staff at my church and President of the PTA at my son's school. I had a strong core group of friends that served as co-parents to Caden and my life was full. That is until I found myself stuck indoors, without any of those things to define me or occupy my time. It was just me and Caden and while he was in his virtual classroom, I was stuck with myself.

For the first time in a long time, I was stuck asking the questions, Who am I? What Now? What Next? How am I doing, REALLY? I had no clue. Beyond quoting scriptures and reciting affirmations, I was at a loss for words. Again, I found myself in a depressive state, but this time with no one to help me out because everyone around me was experiencing their own inner turmoil. As dark as this time was and as hard as it was, this was the time that I learned to say, "I'm Not Okay." It was the first time in 10 years that I was able to give an honest answer of how I am doing. I wish I was standing in front of you so you can see the joy on my face when I describe to you the freedom that came with answering that question honestly for myself. There is freedom in being honest with yourself and others about how you're doing.

Once I was able to say how I'm doing, I was then able to ask myself 'Why am I not okay?' You see, your response determines the next step. Responding honestly helps you or the other person ask the right follow-up questions and begin making connections. The conversation with myself went something like this:

"How are you?"

"I am not okay."

"Why are you not okay?"

"My world has been turned upside down."

"What makes you think your world is turned upside down?"

"I lost my job; I'm no longer engaged in other activities and I don't feel a connection to my friends."

"Wow! I can see why you're not okay. How does that make you feel?"

"I feel like my sense of purpose is gone.

And there it was, the underline feeling that all the other feelings stemmed from: I felt like I lost my sense of purpose. I would have never gotten to that if I wasn't honest with myself in saying that I am not okay and then being willing to unpack that. I know, easier said than done but I think the most important thing is to take the first step which is acknowledging how you really feel; First to yourself and then to those you trust. That's the hardest part. After that you will be surprised at how much you start to unpack and the more you unpack, the lighter you will feel. From there the mapping begins. Overtime your response to the question will go from "I'm not okay" to "I'm doing okay" to "I'm doing great."

So, I ask you, How are you doing? How are you feeling? Not about the meal you cooked last night, or the kids' game or your project at work. No. How are you feeling about yourself?

14

Journal Entry Writing Activity

JOURNALING DAY 1

In what ways did this chapter resonate with you?

_____

_____

_____

_____

_____

_____

_____

_____

_____

_____

_____

_____

_____

_____

_____

_____

_____

_____

_____

Journal Entry Writing Activity

JOURNALING DAY 2

How are you doing, really?

_____

_____

_____

_____

_____

_____

_____

_____

_____

_____

_____

_____

_____

_____

_____

_____

_____

_____

_____

Journal Entry Writing Activity

JOURNALING DAY 3

How honest have you been with others about the way you are feeling?

_____

_____

_____

_____

_____

_____

_____

_____

_____

_____

_____

_____

_____

_____

_____

_____

_____

_____

_____

_____

Journal Entry Writing Activity

JOURNALING DAY 4

Take some time and think back to the moment you decided to focus solely on your child(ren). What was happening at that time?

_____

_____

_____

_____

_____

_____

_____

_____

_____

_____

_____

_____

_____

_____

_____

_____

_____

_____

Journal Entry Writing Activity

JOURNALING DAY 5

Review your journal responses from day 1-4 and write the connections you made based on your responses. What stuck out to you? Were you able to identify an underline problem to explain or validate your feelings?

_____

_____

_____

_____

_____

_____

_____

_____

_____

_____

_____

_____

_____

_____

_____

_____

WEEK 2

Hey Mom

It's Time to Expose the Coverup!

HEY MOM, IT'S TIME TO EXPOSE THE COVERUP!

Years ago, I started Women On Purpose, a faith based organization whose mission is to educate, equip and empower women to walk in their purpose. At one of our Women On Purpose workshops, I had the ladies do an activity that required them to take a very perfect puzzle, pull it apart, write on it, and put it back together. After the activity, we had some time to process and one woman said the hardest thing for her was watching the other women put their pieces back together with seemingly no effort while she's struggling with no one to help. Interestingly enough, I couldn't tell she was struggling to put her pieces together, when I passed by, it appeared that she was moving along perfectly. Many of us can attest to covering up the severity of our situation during difficult seasons which resulted in us feeling like we are alone. This eventually leads to emotional isolation. Socially we're okay, we get dressed up and we present ourselves in a manner that says "all is well" when deep down we're crying out for someone to recognize our inner distress.

There is a scene from the television show, 'How to Get Away with Murder' that resonates with me. In the scene, Annalise is sitting at her vanity in anguish. With a gaze of vulnerability in her eyes, she starts to take off her jewelry. She then takes off her wig, followed by her lashes. She eventually wipes off all her makeup. The scene lasts about one minute but what it represents to all women is a profound message; It represents the removing of the image that we embody every time we leave our sacred space. It's the stripping down of our public persona to the private reality that awaits us. Let me just say, our house is not always our sacred space. For some of us, it's the car, the laundry room, the pantry. For others, it's the dressing room in a department store. For me, it's the bathroom. Your sacred space is anywhere you are free just being. It is the place you go to cry, clear your mind, or just to hideout from the pressures of life. As a mom, we know that sacred space all too well because it's the place we visit to maintain our sanity in the midst of our daily demands.

This public persona has caused us to be excellent undercover agents and skilled operatives. We have become experienced at covering up the truth of our lives. The sad truth is that it's expected that we do. To comment on motherhood being anything short of amazing is to be looked at as a terrible mother. I learned very early how to cover up difficult seasons, I am a pro at that. When Caden was two-years-old I was evicted from my apartment. For two months I lived in hotels and my car. It took almost a month before a friend found out because I had done such a good job to cover it up. I remember one Sunday, after sleeping in my car all night, I called a friend and asked to take a shower at her house. I lied and told her the water in my apartment building had been shut off due to a pipe leak. She never suspected anything, I went over to her house and got ready for church. My friend and mentor Rev. Dr. Natasha Gadson was preaching that day. I wanted to be present to help her in any way. Even though we spoke almost every day, I managed to keep that one detail out.

A few months ago, we were talking, and she mentioned that she came across the picture we took that day and her thoughts reflecting on the moment. Finally, I disclosed to her that the night before that picture we had slept in a hotel parking lot in the car because we could no longer afford to stay anywhere, and I was too ashamed to admit that I was homeless. She was stunned. Other than looking a little tired and the few fly-away hair strands from my ponytail, I was perfectly dressed. I had long mastered the art of covering up the truth of my life, I had done it so many times before. However, in keeping my public image, there were times when I felt like I was going crazy. Times when I just wanted to retreat to a different space, both physically and emotionally. It became so exhausting and emotionally taxing trying to maintain an image that was contrary to my reality. It was hard for me to dream in those times. I was just functioning, trying to get by day-to-day, but I wasn't living. I was suffering in silence. I remember just wanting my situation to improve. That was as far as I could aspire to.

During that time a friend of mine kept asking how I was doing. Each time I would respond and say, "I'm okay." It was all I could muster up. Secretly, I hoped that person would delve deeper, but they never did. One day, that friend said to me, "I notice every time I asked you how you are doing you say okay, we should talk about that one day." I waited for that day to come but it never did. My friend Tasha was the only person I told and that was because she kept pushing. She saw the signs, the bags under my eyes, the weight loss, and the sadness beneath my smile. She kept asking questions. She was tenacious yet patient and showed great care. I can't tell you how relieved I was when I told her. I no longer had to live the nightmare alone. My situation didn't improve by telling her, but my emotional state did. Later I was able to make decisions to improve the situation.

I've heard confessions are good for the soul but bad for the reputation. I must admit I've always had issues with that statement. Yes, there is truth to it, but the reality is we must be mindful of who we confess to and be vulnerable with. You cannot be vulnerable with everybody, but you should be vulnerable with somebody. Most importantly, you must first be honest with yourself. You must admit to yourself that you are in need of help and it doesn't make you any less of a woman or a mother if you accept help. I know it's a hard reality to embrace but I want you to know that we all experience struggle and difficult seasons throughout our lives. It's inevitable. There is no blueprint to struggle nor is there a timeline for how long we go through it and yes it does look different for everyone. Rid yourself of the pressure of being the perfect parent. Call a truce between the public persona and private reality and choose to live out your truth knowing that you are not alone. The way you handle the difficult seasons in your life is sometimes more of a testimony than your words can ever express. Your testimony spoken or lived might be the word someone is waiting for to provide the encouragement they need to get out of their situation. It's time to expose the cover-up.

Journal Entry Writing Activity

JOURNALING DAY 1

In what ways did this chapter resonate with you?

_____

_____

_____

_____

_____

_____

_____

_____

_____

_____

_____

_____

_____

_____

_____

_____

_____

Journal Entry Writing Activity

JOURNALING DAY 2

Write about a difficult situation or season that you have experienced. Did you cover it up from those around you? What did you learn from the way you handled the situation? In hindsight, would you have done anything differently?

_____

_____

_____

_____

_____

_____

_____

_____

_____

_____

_____

_____

_____

_____

_____

_____

Journal Entry Writing Activity

JOURNALING DAY 3

What are some internal struggles that you have been coping with silently? How have you been coping with it?

Journal Entry Writing Activity

JOURNALING DAY 4

Is there someone in your life that you can confide in? What qualities does that person possess that qualifies them to be a confidant?

_____

_____

_____

_____

_____

_____

_____

_____

_____

_____

_____

_____

_____

_____

_____

_____

_____

Journal Entry Writing Activity

JOURNALING DAY 5

How can you be sensitive to the struggles of those around you?

_____

_____

_____

_____

_____

_____

_____

_____

_____

_____

_____

_____

_____

_____

_____

_____

_____

_____

_____

Hey Mom,
IT'S TIME TO EXPOSE THE COVER-UP!

—

Hey Mom

You're Not in This By Yourself

HEY MOM, YOU'RE NOT IN THIS BY YOURSELF

One of the worst feelings in life is being lonely-- particularly in difficult times. Please note, I am not speaking about being alone, being in solitude, or enjoying your own company. There's a difference between choosing to be alone and feeling your only choice is loneliness.

Loneliness is feeling like no one understands you. It's when you believe if you tell others about your situation, people would judge you. I used to think only single moms experience loneliness. However, I learned all moms experience it. Last year, I met with one of Caden's friends and his mom for a play date. While the boys were playing, we sat talking. She shared insight that was taking place in her life and I did the same. To her surprise, she said, "I never thought someone like you would experience that". Oh, the assumptions we make of others! She went on to say, "You're a minister, you're always well put-together and you walk around like everything is fine." That day we both learned that our lives weren't as different as it seemed on the outside.

You know the mom you look at and think, 'One day I want to be just like her?' Chances are she's either looking at you thinking the same thing or she's looking at you making assumptions of her own. Societal pressures make us feel like if we haven't figured it all out and we're not enjoying every minute of motherhood we must be doing something wrong. So, naturally, we look at the mom who seemingly checks all the boxes and we compare ourselves to her with little to no context or insight into her life. One mom said to me, "Tanna, whenever you have the kids for playdates, you always do fun things with them. When I have them, I just let them run around the house." My response to her was, "I do that because I have a small apartment so in order to keep from losing my mind, I take them out each time. However, if I had a mini-mansion (as my son refers to her house) like you with a huge backyard, I would let them run around too."

Another mom said to me, "Tanna, you're always so organized." She said this in response to me sharing the details of my plans for a trip to the amusement park for our kids. What she didn't know was I was organized so that I could manage the cost of the trip as money was tight at the time. Yet even in my meticulous planning, I forgot to pack a meal for myself and ended up having to spend an additional $50 in the park that day.

Another mom said to me, "Tanna, you're such a good mom, you're always volunteering at Caden's school." Yes, I am very intentional about scheduling time to volunteer and support Caden in school but when this mom made her comment I was only working part-time and I didn't have a car. It was easier to volunteer at Caden's school than to keep going back and forth on the bus and train.

Part of the loneliness we feel comes from the assumptions we make of others. It then makes us isolated in our experiences because that other person couldn't possibly understand what we're going through. The reality is quite the opposite. I'm not saying that we all experience the same thing, I'm saying that there is more that connects us than separates us, but we have to take the time to make the connection.

Every time I make an assumption of someone I eventually have a conversation with, I leave with a different take. It's not that my assumptions were wrong, it's just we had more in common than I originally thought.

More than reading a good book with a cup of coffee, I like reading a book with a book club or small group. It's something about hearing each person's take on a subject or sharing related stories that fuels conversation, brings understanding, and eventually creates commonality. It's the reason why I asked you in the introduction to get a reading partner or start a book club. If for nothing else, to let you know that you are not by yourself on this journey called motherhood, your feelings are valid, and they are shared.

Journal Entry Writing Activity

JOURNALING DAY 1

When do you feel the most alone? What is happening around you to make you feel that way?

_____

_____

_____

_____

_____

_____

_____

_____

_____

_____

_____

_____

_____

_____

_____

_____

Journal Entry Writing Activity

JOURNALING DAY 2

Who is someone you look at and think, 'I wish I could be like them' or 'they have it all together'? What assumptions have you made about that person?

_____

_____

_____

_____

_____

_____

_____

_____

_____

_____

_____

_____

_____

_____

_____

_____

_____

_____

_____

Journal Entry Writing Activity

JOURNALING DAY 3

What assumptions have others made about you? How does it make you feel when people make assumptions?

_____

_____

_____

_____

_____

_____

_____

_____

_____

_____

_____

_____

_____

_____

_____

_____

Journal Entry Writing Activity

JOURNALING DAY 4

What changes can you make to avoid falling into seasons of loneliness?

_____

_____

_____

_____

_____

_____

_____

_____

_____

_____

_____

_____

_____

_____

_____

_____

_____

Journal Entry Writing Activity

JOURNALING DAY 5

Imagine that someone has asked you to speak to a group of moms about yourself and your experience as a mom. Write either talking points or your full speech.

_____

_____

_____

_____

_____

_____

_____

_____

_____

_____

_____

_____

_____

_____

_____

_____

_____

_____

_____

Hey Mom,
YOU'RE NOT IN THIS BY YOURSELF

WEEK 4

—

Hey Mom

You Passed the Rest Stop

HEY MOM, YOU PASSED THE REST STOP

A few years ago, I offered to drive my mom to a wedding she was attending in Columbia, South Carolina. It was a seven and a half-hour drive and up until that point I had only driven a maximum of six hours (two of those hours were from sitting in traffic). But, I thought, 'Hey, what is one and a half more hours.

We got on the road a lot later than intended and I began my commute around 4 pm, at the onset of rush hour. The first few hours were fine, however as I hit the fourth hour, I began to get tired. I reached for a snack and queued up my favorite playlist. My mom suggested that I stopped to rest but I insisted on only stopping when she or Caden needed to use the restroom. We hit multiple blocks of traffic and an accident extended the drive another two hours. On the final stretch to the hotel, close to midnight a thunderstorm hit. I tried to keep driving but between exhaustion, a backache, and being on a highway with nothing but tractor trailers, I finally decided to pull over.

Fast forward two days, the wedding is over, and it's time to drive back. I had an obligation the next morning and decided to hop on the road to drive back home immediately after the wedding reception. We got on the road about 10 pm and I drove through the night. Oh, what a night! I was so exhausted, and my back was hurting terribly. We made it back around 7 am, I rested for about an hour before preparing to head back out.

I'm sure you're tired just reading this.

Even as I write this, I'm shaking my head in disbelief and disappointment that I pushed myself that hard. What disappoints me is that I didn't have to, but the "I'm Every Woman, It's All In Me" soundtrack was playing in my head. Please hear me when I say this, just because you can do something, doesn't always mean you should. In hindsight, I shouldn't have obligated myself to be somewhere when I knew I was heading out of town. That would have meant that I could stay an extra night and rest before getting on the road. I should have prioritized rest above all else knowing the danger a lack of it could pose to myself and others. I also needed to utilize the rest stops instead, I bypassed them all. By the time I did stop, we were on the final stretch home and I just couldn't go anymore without resting.

Isn't that the same for many of us? We wait until our bodies are at the point of giving up completely before we stop and rest. To make matters worse, we use every quiet moment as a time to do pending tasks. And why wouldn't we? It's the best time to get things done. It's quiet and we are at our most productive at those times. But what about after? What about after the kids wake up or return home refueled with energy? What then? How are you appearing to your kids in those weary moments? Are you temperamental? Do you lash out at them? Are you vetoing every request they make? I can confess that I have displayed each of the aforementioned when I am tired. The look on Caden's face in those moments would bring me a pang of guilt and sadness. Even then, rather than adjust my behavior, I started overcompensating for it. I bought more toys, more kids meals, and pushed bedtime back. I did any and everything to keep him happy at the moment except the one thing that would last, parenting at my best.

At a very early age when Caden noticed a change in my behavior, he would give me a hug and say, "Mommy I think you should sit down and take a break." Without me saying what was wrong Caden was able to identify the problem and extend grace. I tear up every time I reflect on those moments.

Societal pressures make us think that we must keep busy in order to be deemed "a good parent" but being a good parent is knowing when to stop and rest. Understand that motion doesn't always equal productivity; Just because we're busy, doesn't mean we're producing positive results. The goal should never be to be busy rather, to be efficient. In order to do that, you must be intentional about prioritizing the things on your schedule with rest being non-negotiable.

Let me note that rest doesn't necessarily mean sleep though sleeping is simply one way to rest. Rest can include ten minutes of sitting in silence, a short walk, watching your favorite tv show, or doing any activity that gives you peace of mind. Before you go throwing a guilt trip on yourself for desiring to do any of those things, let me tell you that according to the dictionary, rest is characterized as a verb. If you can remember your elementary school lessons, you'll recall that a verb is an action word. So, don't allow anyone to let you feel guilty for "doing nothing", resting is doing something. It's probably the most productive thing you can do because it fuels you to do all the other things.

Mom, don't miss the rest stop!

Journal Entry Writing Activity

JOURNALING DAY 1

What does rest currently look like for you?

_____

_____

_____

_____

_____

_____

_____

_____

_____

_____

_____

_____

_____

_____

_____

Journal Entry Writing Activity

JOURNALING DAY 2

LIST THINGS YOU ENJOY DOING.	WHEN WAS THE LAST TIME YOU DID IT?	HOW OFTEN HAVE YOU DONE IT?

HOW CAN YOU BE INTENTIONAL ABOUT MAKING TIME FOR THE THINGS YOU ENJOY DOING?

_____

_____

_____

_____

_____

_____

_____

_____

_____

_____

_____

_____

Journal Entry Writing Activity

JOURNALING DAY 3

LIST ALL YOUR DEPENDENTS	LIST THE THINGS THAT POUR INTO YOU.

HOW CAN YOU BALANCE THAT LIST?

_____

_____

_____

_____

_____

_____

_____

_____

_____

_____

_____

_____

_____

Journal Entry Writing Activity

JOURNALING DAY 4

How can you be more intentional about resting? What are some things you can do to remind you to rest? (E.g. set an alarm on your phone, block off time in your calendar specifically to do a restful activity)

_____

_____

_____

_____

_____

_____

_____

_____

_____

_____

_____

_____

_____

_____

practice

REST TODAY

Hey Mom,

YOU PASSED THE REST STOP

—

Hey Mom

Let's Prioritize You

———

HEY MOM, LET'S PRIORITIZE YOU

Somewhere in his pre-kindergarten year, Caden became obsessed with sequential order. At the start of every day Caden wanted me to list everything, we were doing that day. Once I did it, he would take my list and place it in an order that benefitted him. The conversation would go something like this:

Caden: "Mommy, what are we doing today?"

Me: "I need to get gas, stop at Target and pick up a few things, drop off my dry cleaning, take you to the park for a playdate, and swing by the grocery store to pick up something for dinner."

Caden: "Ok, First, we stop at Target." – It's his favorite store.

"Second, we go to the park for a play date." - Chances are he'll talk me into buying a toy at Target, so naturally he wants to show it to his friends.

"Third, we get gas" - He will probably ask me to run in and buy him a snack.

"Fourth, we go to the grocery store" - He will probably ask for a donut from the bakery.

"Fifth, we go to the dry cleaners" - Nothing benefits him at the dry cleaners.

———

This was a daily conversation. Of course, it was easier on school or camp days. No matter what variation of a to-do list I threw at him, he managed to make it benefit him in some way and to rearrange it in a way that prioritized his needs. I was always intrigued by Caden's ability to do that. We know that kids have a selfish streak because they're born with a dependence on us and they grow accustomed to being the center of attention. From their first cry, they taught us to prioritize them and to tend to their needs in a timely manner.

I remember my first few nights with Caden once we got home from the hospital. I was a single parent and doing this alone. Naturally, he woke up every two hours to be fed and changed. Each time I got up to feed and change him it would take me some time to fall back asleep. As soon as I would go back to sleep, he would be up and crying again. By the third or fourth time this happened, I started crying right along with him. I was so exhausted. Eventually, my body adjusted to his schedule and life went on.

As Caden got older our night and day schedules changed and we adjusted. Caden knew I dropped him off at the daycare when I needed to go to work. He knew I dropped him off at the nursery when we were at church. He knew what time we went to bed and he knew what days were set aside for play dates and the park. What he didn't know was, a time set aside for me to rest or do things I enjoyed doing. I adjusted my world completely to revolve around him. I stopped meeting up with friends, I fell into a rut and used Caden as the reason I couldn't do anything outside of work and church. If Caden couldn't go somewhere, I wasn't going. So Caden never learned that mommy needed a break or mommy needed time to herself. He never learned that mommy too needed to be prioritized. I know there's a thin line between prioritizing yourself and being selfish. I am not at all suggesting the latter, but I am saying that we can teach our children, our loved ones, how to prioritize ourselves.

A few years ago, I planned a trip to a nearby theme park for Caden and his friend. I knew the trip would cost a lot, so I bought the tickets months in advance and prepared over time. In the days leading up to the trip I combed through the website so I could familiarize myself with the park and its offerings. I printed the map and our tickets, purchased parking passes, and determined where we were going to park. I determined our arrival and departure times and reviewed them with the other mom. With my meticulous planning, we were the second family to arrive at the park which meant the kids rode countless rides before the lines started forming. They had a blast. We spent about 7 hours there. After leaving the park, we went to a nearby restaurant before getting on the road. While at the restaurant, I noticed one of my favorite stores, so after eating, we went in for a few minutes. The kids looked annoyed and my son said to me, "Why do we have to come here?" I said to him, "The entire day was spent doing what you enjoyed doing and I never complained, now I'm asking for 20 minutes to do something I enjoy doing." I didn't need to explain any further, he understood what I was saying and turned to his friend and said, "My mom is just having some shopping time, let's be patient with her." They followed me around the store playing quietly with one another and waiting patiently. About 20 minutes later, we got back on the highway and headed home.

You might be saying, 'What did 20 minutes do for you?' Well, it made me forget about waking up at 4 am to get us ready, pick up his friend and then drive two and a half hours to the theme park. It made me forget about the long day at the park going from ride to ride, keeping track of two kids in a crowded park, and getting on rides I didn't want to get on. It made me forget that I had to spend an additional 100 dollars at the park to purchase a locker, food, and souvenirs. It made me forget that I had to drive another two and a half hours to get us back home. Twenty minutes allowed me to just breathe as I browsed through my favorite store and that 20 minutes fueled me for the rest of the evening.

That was the first of many lessons I taught Caden. I informed him that I would prioritize him and ensure he had the best experiences, however, I would do the same for me. When your children see you making time to prioritize yourself, pamper yourself, pour into yourself, they begin to conceptualize the idea of you needing to be prioritized. I knew we were making strides when Caden said to me one day, "My friend and I want to have a play date on Saturday and we already asked his mom. You can drop me off and have the day to yourself." Aside from the fact that he made plans without first consulting me, Caden figured out a way to prioritize his need and mine, in a way that was most beneficial and enjoyable for us both.

Hey Mom, it's time to teach others to prioritize you. It's time to prioritize yourself.

Journal Entry Writing Activity

JOURNALING DAY 1

In what ways did this chapter resonate with you?

_____

_____

_____

_____

_____

_____

_____

_____

_____

_____

_____

_____

_____

_____

_____

_____

Journal Entry Writing Activity

JOURNALING DAY 2

How intentional have you been with prioritizing yourself?

_____

_____

_____

_____

_____

_____

_____

_____

_____

_____

_____

_____

_____

_____

Journal Entry Writing Activity

JOURNALING DAY 3

What are some adjustments you can make to ensure you prioritize yourself?

_____

_____

_____

_____

_____

_____

_____

_____

_____

_____

_____

_____

_____

_____

_____

_____

_____

Journal Entry Writing Activity

JOURNALING DAY 4

How can you teach others to prioritize you? How can you teach your children to prioritize you?

_____

_____

_____

_____

_____

_____

_____

_____

_____

_____

_____

_____

_____

_____

_____

_____

Journal Entry Writing Activity

JOURNALING DAY 5

What will prioritizing yourself look like? Imagine a day that you were intentional about prioritizing yourself. Describe the day.

_____

_____

_____

_____

_____

_____

_____

_____

_____

_____

_____

_____

_____

_____

_____

_____

_____

_____

Hey Mom, LET'S PRIORITIZE

WEEK 6

—

Hey Mom

It's Okay to Take Care of You

HEY MOM, IT'S OKAY TO TAKE CARE OF YOU

One morning, I made breakfast for Caden and got him ready for virtual learning. A few hours later he came out of his room for lunch. I prepared his meal and gave it to him. While eating, he noticed I was a little spaced out in my responses to him and asked if I was okay. I let him know I was fine, I just hadn't eaten yet. Caden said to me, "Mommy you know it's okay to put yourself first sometimes? You don't have to put everyone before you." That conversation, with my then 9-year-old, inspired the title of this book.

It was the reminder I needed. I spent the entire morning without stopping to eat. I prepared breakfast, lunch, and a snack for Caden answered numerous emails and made several phone calls. One might say, "Well maybe you weren't hungry" but the fact is, I was very hungry. By the time Caden shared that insight with me, I started to get a headache and I felt disoriented. As much as I would like to say this was a rare occasion, it wasn't. It was a constant occurrence.

You see, I am that person who is always doing way too much. I'm that person you can ask to do one thing and I turn around and do that plus, ten other things because I want to make your life easier. I'm the person who attends a wedding as a guest and by the end of the wedding everyone is asking if I am the wedding planner because I'm running around ensuring everything works out smoothly. I do this for every event I'm invited to. It got so bad that I stopped accepting invitations because I wouldn't trust myself to just attend and have a good time. So, when I became a parent that was already my default setting. Parenting only magnified what was already there; the need to care for others and go above and beyond at all times. The thing is I wouldn't allow others to do the same for me and worst, I didn't do it for myself.

When I was invited to apply for my position as Regional Program Manager at the organization I was previously employed with, I had two very important conversations: one with Caden and the other with my friend Tasha. The position was supervisory and spanned across 4 states which required frequent travel. I sat Caden down and told him about the opportunity and the impact it would have on our lives. I would no longer be able to volunteer as much at his school, he would have to spend the night at his aunts from time to time, and occasionally I would have to drop him to school earlier than usual or pick him up later than usual. After telling him this, Caden said to me, "Mommy, you've already done enough. You don't have to always be around. I'll be okay and everyone else will be okay."

I had a similar conversation with my friend Tasha. One evening, while on the phone with her, she said, "Tanna, you've made so many sacrifices over the years, as a mom and on the behalf of others. I don't want you to let this opportunity pass because you're worried about the sacrifices others will now have to make for you." My conversation with Tasha unearthed the feelings I had and was too afraid to acknowledge. I didn't want others making sacrifices on my behalf. I thought it was selfish of me. For the next few days, I wrestled with those conversations and the feelings associated with them. I eventually decided to move forward. And guess what? Everyone adjusted. It was a great experience that helped me to be a better parent. It brought a much needed balance to my life in a way I never imagined. When I was on travel, I was able to use the time I would spend with Caden, getting ready for school, doing homework, cooking dinner, etc. to do things I enjoyed doing. I took walks, I read books, I slept in, I spent time in prayer, and I rested. Every time I returned home, I was happier, rested, and relaxed which allowed for me to enjoy Caden so much more.

I hope by now you understand the importance of taking care of yourself. I know it seems impossible at times, but you must be intentional about taking care of yourself so you can be a better version of yourself and for those you love. God created us as nurturers. However, the nurturing must first be inward and then spread outwards. For so long we've had it backwards. My prayer is that you will begin to reverse that and find a balance that works for everyone including YOU.

Mom, it's okay to take care of you!

Journal Entry Writing Activity

JOURNALING DAY 1

What are some take-aways you got from the book?

_____

_____

_____

_____

_____

_____

_____

_____

_____

_____

_____

_____

_____

_____

_____

_____

_____

_____

Activity: Tree of Fulfillment

Branches: Write the names of the people that are dependent on you (children, spouse, etc.)

Trunk: List your support systems

Ground: List the things that keep you grounded

After filling in the spaces, take your colored pencils and draw leaves on the tree based on how you feel presently as a parent. E.g. If you feel fulfilled draw a tree that is full and vibrant. If you feel depleted, your tree might only have a few leaves on it. If you feel half or partially fulfilled, then the tree will only have half of its leaves.

Journal Entry Writing Activity

JOURNALING DAY 3

How has your tree changed since the start of the book?

_____

_____

_____

_____

_____

_____

_____

_____

_____

_____

_____

_____

_____

_____

_____

Journal Entry Writing Activity

JOURNALING DAY 4

What's next? What behaviors will you change immediately? What behaviors will you be intentional about changing over time?

_____

_____

_____

_____

_____

_____

_____

_____

_____

_____

_____

_____

_____

_____

_____

_____

_____

_____

_____

Journal Entry Writing Activity

JOURNALING DAY 5

Is there a mom you could tell about the book and the things you've learned? What would you say to her? How can you use what you've learned in the book to help other moms?

_____

_____

_____

_____

_____

_____

_____

_____

_____

_____

_____

_____

_____

_____

_____

_____

HEY MOM,

IT'S OKAY TO TAKE CARE OF YOU

Take Care

A PERSONAL WORD

———

Four years ago, I started writing this book, but never committed to it. When 2020 arrived and we were thrust into a pandemic the book came to mind and I decided to complete and publish it. I would be remised if I didn't tell you after writing the book, I felt hypocritical. Although each chapter has an anecdote from my life experiences, I must confess that all the strides I made to get to a place of taking care of myself went down the drain when we entered a state of nationwide quarantine amidst the pandemic. I could not, in good conscience, end the book without acknowledging the challenges the pandemic brought to our daily lives especially as it relates to our families. Many of us found ourselves homeschooling or as IT assistants to our kids. We were comforting our children when in fact we needed comforting ourselves. We were trying to explain to our children what was happening when in fact we didn't really know. There was no breathing time while the kids were away at school/daycare, swimming lessons, etc. In an instant, our realities shifted with no advance warning. I want you to know I've felt it with you. For those parenting alone or feeling like you're parenting alone, I know the effects are double and the support is even more limited than usual. I believe the first step is acknowledging that.

We are indeed in what the news outlets have coined "unprecedented times". It's important to take some time to grieve that reality if you haven't already done so (it took me six months, prayerfully it wouldn't be that long for you). Second, extend grace: to yourself first, then to your children, spouse, family, and friends. We are all trying to figure this out.

In the first month of the shutdown, I remember getting so upset with Caden because I kept tripping over his toys in the living room. The living room was never tidy because his toys were everywhere and that frustrated me. It made my environment feel cluttered at a time when my mind was already cluttered and it felt like there was no clear space around me, physically, emotionally, or mentally. What I came to realize was Caden brought his toys to the living room because that's where I spent most of my day and he wanted to be around me. I was the only one he could be around since we were in quarantine. Once I recognized that I was able to extend grace to him. As I sit at the table typing this, I look into my living room and it is cluttered with toys. However, I am reminded that he wants to be close to me. Also, I am looking for a new place, with a basement (inserts eyewink).

Lastly, get creative. I believe the principles in this book can be effective, but it requires creative thinking at a time like this. It's also a good time to teach those around you how to care for you. The same way you teach your kids how to care for a new baby or how to adjust to an ailing grandparent, you can teach them how to take care of you.

Often, around the time Caden's favorite show comes on, I fix him a snack and make everything accessible I think he might need. Before the show starts, I say to him, "Caden, I'm about to take a few minutes to myself in my room. On the table you will find... on the center table, you will find...I'll be out by 4:00." I give him a set time because it helps his patience when he knows how long he has to wait. During that time, I do whatever I want to do-- read, sleep, listen to music, etc.

Another thing I do to care for myself is wake up early. It gives me time to drink my coffee, pray, and meditate in silence. Since I'm a morning person, I try to go to sleep early to get an adequate amount of rest. It helps bring a positive start to my day.

I'll confess there are a lot of things I would like to do but I haven't figured out how to do them yet. As I keep my creative juices flowing, in due time I will unlock a new idea. If you have any ideas of your own feel free to reach out to me and share some of your ideas. I would love to hear them and share them with others. My dream is to create a community of support, encouragement, and empowerment for women in all walks of life.

Visit

TANNAABRAHAM.COM

Other Activities

SELF-CARE IDEAS

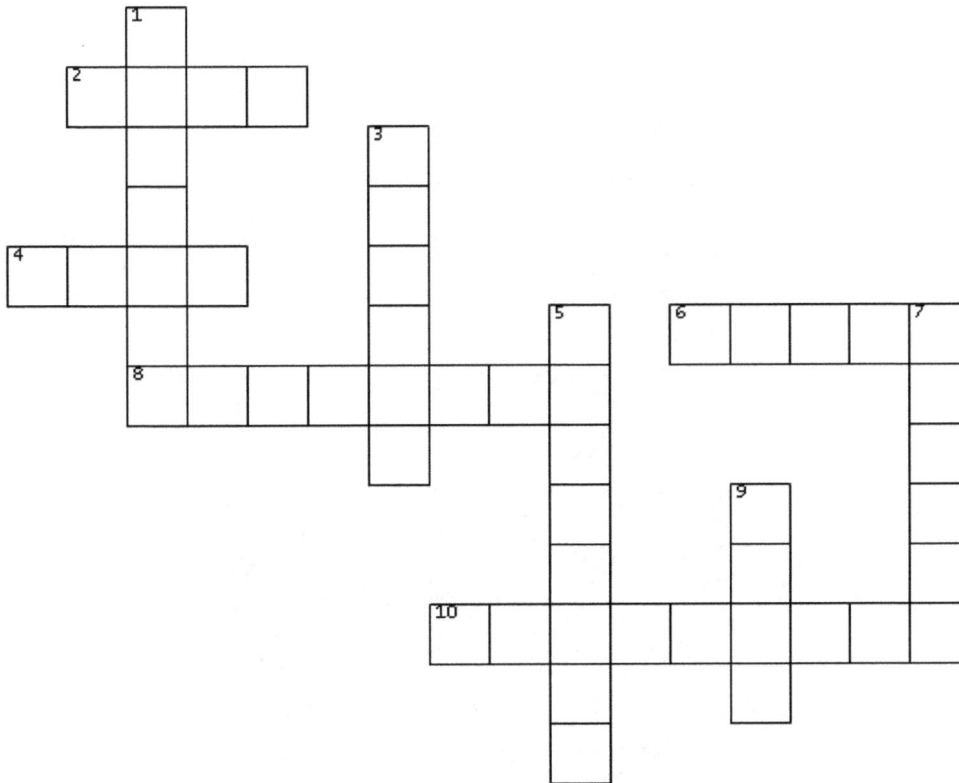

ACROSS

2. BEST DONE OUTDOORS AT YOUR OWN PACE
4. GRAB YOUR FAVORITE BOOK AND DO THIS
6. CUE UP YOUR FAVORITE PLAYLIST AND LISTEN
8. PHYSICAL ACTIVITY TO IMPROVE YOUR HEALTH AND FITNESS
10. BEING THANKFUL FOR ALL YOU HAVE

DOWN

1. RELIEVES THE TENSION IN YOUR BODY AS YOU LAY/SIT AND LISTEN TO SOOTHING SOUNDS
3. A COMBINATION OF TWO MEALS, CAN BE ENJOYED WITH A GROUP OF FRIENDS
5. FOCUS YOUR MIND ON SOMETHING POSITIVE FOR A PERIOD OF TIME
7. LIGHT THIS AND ALLOW THE AROMA TO FILL THE ROOM
9. IMMERSING IN A TUB OF WATER FOR A LONG PERIOD OF TIME WHILE ALSO CLEANING YOUR BODY

WORD SEARCH

W	Z	F	W	N	W	K	D	E	H	D	A	E	J	D
E	W	O	E	C	J	D	E	R	X	E	V	T	Z	Z
Y	C	H	L	S	T	T	U	U	F	O	Y	F	O	U
K	F	Q	L	R	U	D	G	T	L	Z	T	M	I	X
J	T	E	N	L	I	K	S	R	P	Z	F	L	O	A
I	M	Q	E	N	A	Z	K	U	B	N	Y	J	F	M
B	Z	Z	S	B	Z	Y	G	N	P	B	N	X	V	P
Z	X	X	S	R	N	A	G	C	X	P	Y	M	J	Y
E	M	P	O	W	E	R	M	E	N	T	O	F	D	S
W	U	B	T	D	U	H	I	X	B	N	T	R	K	Q
C	W	X	Y	Q	P	M	T	X	Y	C	S	Z	T	H
E	R	A	C	F	L	E	S	O	I	C	E	I	H	E
J	H	O	K	K	Z	K	J	T	M	Y	R	N	S	W
T	N	E	M	L	L	I	F	L	U	F	O	U	H	N
B	A	L	A	N	C	E	G	U	L	D	T	J	V	Z

BALANCE   **JOY**   **REST**
EMPOWER   **LOVE**   **SELFCARE**
FULFILLMENT   **MOTHERS**   **SUPPORT**
HEYMOM   **NURTURE**   **WELLNESS**